Letter to Country

Letter to Country

Poems by

Rethabile Masilo

CANOPIC
PUBLISHING

Canopic Publishing
389 Lincoln Ave
Woodstock, IL 60098
www.canopicpublishing.com

Virginia Smith Rice, Editor

Book design by Phil Rice
Cover design by Georges Stratan
Cover art © Bram Janssens

First edition

   p. cm.
 ISBN-13: 978-0-9971695-2-2 (alk. paper)
 ISBN-10: 0-9971695-2-4 (alk. paper)

Printed in the United States of America
5 4 3 2 1

For mother, sisters, country

Contents

Letter to Country

Places & People

A park in Clocolan

My grandfather also liked to tell the story
of a baobab that pushed away asphalt
and grew, though they kept cutting it
and covering its stump with tar.

And each time it would grow stronger
and push with more passion. Seven times
they sawed it, poured plant poison on it
and shovelled tar onto its fresh wound.

But it was saved by providence and guts,
and it came back again and again, against
their bricks and their mortar, dug in now
and getting angrier each time. In the end
the government had to make that street
swerve around her, like a private ring road.

When she was old enough and tired
of breathing the fumes of civilisation,
they grew grass around her, put a painted
bench there and installed a water fountain
that had a sign that said *blankes* on it.

The journeying poem

—*for Pamela Mordecai*

Every time words fall into the crystal of my poem
I'm startled, what once was a wish to set down
a part of life, and the course of it, an encounter
with the devil, faces of politicians in smug
empires, turns to reality. I move with chimes
that come from a humble morning *hi,* and again
with the neighbour's own version of it when it comes
floating back. I sail on the subway and stop
where the wind is dying, and a sign shouts STOP
to the startled dark. I know when words have fallen
into place because the seam is gone between you
and life, my voice, my fear of failing; and because
time must unhang each of the bodies dangling
from the branch; they have done their time; let
the poem spread over the valley and sing to the sun
the song of remedy, till I harness it and tell it
not to think so much. Ad-lib, I tell it. Fall like snow
in the Kalahari, rise like water up the 'Maletsunyane falls,
jump above life like Thabana Ntlenyana. But the poem
is getting tired, and closes an eye, like a child
being read to at bedtime, and finally, another eye.

Paris to Maryville

The trains of Paris pull out, pull in
all the time, and because I'm on a platform with a bag
I exist everywhere. People look at me and wonder
what kind of destination is written on my face.
Many of them run by in a flurry
even before the siren rings. I could chase them
if I wanted to, but I'm an old cat
and in no hurry at all. I'll stand here
like a person waiting for some passenger,
studying the face of every passer-by.
If you look at me once I'll always remember
having seen your eyes before, after all
don't good things come to those who wait?
If the station-master hadn't made eyes at me
I could have sworn he had
his own lady back home. *Alors… merci, mec,*
pour une telle attention. But I'm here waiting
for a train to carry me across the Atlantic
through Canada, and maybe Chicago, to go
see my woman down in Tennessee.

Appalachia

We sit on the porch; sleepers, gnats, surround our air,
we are from where there is no past, everyone's
long been away; only you and I remain behind;
when we go to church we sit on opposite ends
of the altar, to see blood take form from each side;
our pastor says there's life after this, says it's good
we'll soon be with god. But I have misgivings, now.
I think nothing of it; I no longer fiddle with time.
When the milkman comes we know it's Monday;
while he gives the fridge milk we stay stout like cadavers,
though he makes screen doors scream at the hinge;
but it's soon time to go to sleep—or to the bathroom—
we rise like grey people.
                            Neighbours come sometimes
with packets of chips, whose salt flakes we hold
in the mouth to soften with saliva, then pour
gin tots behind. On a day like this, when
even the gnats have gone back to their houses
and the odd cock crows in the middle of a morning,
we'll sit here till we have to get back in. Sleep comes
rushing with the scream of an approaching train.

Following the sun

Late in an afternoon whose sun was balanced
on the balustrade of evening, I walked with you
through the city toward it, as iron curtains
clanged at our heels. You held my hand
and led me through each street toward the west,
down that escarpment to the train station,
and beyond it to the Mohokare river, from where
we could see the last yellow fragments of a sun
going to South Africa—just like people
we have been losing to the mines; like diamonds;
like water that slopes down Senqu and its tributaries
carrying the black soil of our hills and the blood
of our mountains; like the conquered territories
across the border up to Mangaung, atop Thabure;
like brains which have been draining across the bridge
thinking of another life. You say nothing, but walk
behind the trail as a hunter follows
a wounded beast, as if by doing so time itself
could be effaced, and we would suddenly be
before all these happenings, with Moshoeshoe
still there, before history, before you and me,
and annexations, Seheri, Motuba and Motlatsi,
but chiefly, before the events of nineteen seventy.

Morning song

Suddenly I felt awkward, and walked off, left heaven
and its Messiah lectures and that flock of sheep,
went down along old rail-tracks past neon signs
whose 'Welcome' flickers at the world,
beyond platforms reserved for new arrivals,
breathing the night air, toward my brother's—
his door was locked, and no reggae was playing;
then to my sister's: too quiet, no smell of food.
I headed to mum's but dared not get her out of bed,
for the hour was ungodly. So I called our dog
and made him chase his tail until morning,
whereupon a sun opened the eyes of all the plants
and started to untie their hands with its light,
each reaching for the nearest trumpet flower.
They played with the birds a song so soft,
your heart bloomed. My siblings came out to hear,
and upon seeing me, threw their hands in the air,
wondering how on earth I had made it back
from the life I had been living, so far from home.
'The folks there were taking my soul away,' I said.
'And that is why I came back from the dead'.

Wherever I will be

When I am sick and dying, gripped by death's hand
and dreading the colour of each day and each night,
a road will open up to take me away,
and I will be happy on it, content that something
as bleak as itself was concerned for my relief,
happy as finding a mother's hands at birth.
There can be no fear of hell on my part,
for no man dreads unicorns and dragons,
it is my children who are the hell of my heart,

because, after the ceremonies, when the women
have retired to go prepare the meals, and men
in song are filling up the grave, wherever I will be
at that time, I shall burn for them. I drink the soup
I am given because there is nothing to yearn for;
gone are the days of wonder when I walked
up and down my city with hope in each step;

spring lived in my limbs then, and green
were the colours of my thoughts, many of which
I harbour still, but which have now turned dour.
I'll keep the memory of time on earth with them,
in the eternity I face, following my last hour.

Once together

—for Julie

The Appalachian autumn of trees stretches out
to where the eye is unable to see, its mélange
of red and yellow the valley's cauldron of hearts
whose blood spatters into nearby, adjacent fields.
Two foals used to roam here, but it's empty
now, save for the forest's fundamental loss. Soon
the blanched ash of winter will overwhelm them,
and death over life will be but momentary again.
A seed waits in the underlying soil, breathing in
and breathing out through the nose, wondering
if it will soon be time to chance a glance outside
and look for the other seed. They had always
been together to graze and gallop up and down
these mountains. Far away, a colt with spread-out
limbs lands on tar and looks around, neighs her name,
calls her many times, like his mother seeking him
when she thought him lost at a show in Knoxville,
knows inexorably that he will find his friend again.
He scratches the asphalt with his hoof and snorts.
Wind had taken him thus, in a seed, and flung him
away even as his girlfriend was burrowing a hole
in the soft grass of the mountain to hunker down
from the fire of what was trying to destroy them.
Her head pokes out of the ash like a snowdrop,
her eyes glistening. Behind a hillock where they
used to sit there is nothing. The naked boughs
discomfit her. Snow begins to brush her face.

On reading 'Elegy for Ferguson'

It is a poem robed in a coat of many
kinds, dark-dyed never to stain, its life
in the hands of both warp and weft.
I saw when I read it again how hands
should be raised only in victory. And,
washed in that vision, all of my hands
fell, became unhigh and not open
to misinterpretation. I will raise them
to hold the poem's placard to the world
in towns up and down this country
to picket the thought of casual killings,
hold it the same way parents hold
newborns to the moon after birth,
and name them, hold it like garlic
inside a haunted house, read from it
in dark corners of my life, summon it,
as one does troops into action, its lore
like the mountains, with the sun low
behind our backs, marching into battle.
Because of your eyes of adversity,
your fire-power, the cold steelness
of your execution, you couldn't have
inherited the gold of Ghana, leader
of our free world, the elephant power
that Takrur made meek even as slaves
were being captured toward Ferguson,
Kingston, San Miguel, you couldn't have
inherited it, because inside the very halls
of your government today are women
and men who make sounds like the hulls
of trading boats emptied of our souls.

Our road

How deep is deep,
which part is dark?
What depth keeps
secrets, and will
some shady dim-
ness suffice to turn
a secret grim?
I'd like to know
if it is this that
I've carried
like a prayer mat
all my life; it
enters me from
nowhere, as we
set off from home
for my kids' school.
From where we live
to where school is
it is merely a five-
minute walk that
often-times turns
to a nightmare.
I have concerns
that someone's out
to spill blood, drive
us out of here.
We would arrive
late if we changed
circuits, and would
have given up,
which is no good.
For this is our road.

King

They've covered miles of terrain between Selma
and Montgomery, walking in an exodus from fire
that burns us. It is like there will be no other chance
for them to walk again, bear down on the doors
of town hall positioned between phallic pillars,
as the heat of the sun fails to deliver what suns
are meant to share, behind the back of the march,
now out of Alabama and onward unto Tennessee
and beyond to the Carolinas—a whole world walks
with them, bundled in wishes and demands they carry
on their shoulders, till at last they climb the stairs
and drop their concerns at the door. For dogs and boots
have no way of stopping that kind of gift, the diversity
in their one face, not hoses and not even knuckles
or spit can change anything. And since that door
is locked, they make a gate into the next century.
The rest of the story is what would finally unfold.

In my village

an old woman's face
is kohlrabi; her piss
washes the world
with holy water;
her spit covers
itself with the dust
of our country.
Atop the snake
of her bent back
a head is perched;
when she's glad
a coccyx wiggles.
Her skull cap
was blown off
by a heart thief,
until after a while
she took things
into her hands
and loved earth
more than men.
Laughter and smiles
carry the aura
of her people. She
says that loving
sometimes returns
at the very end.

A poem starting with a line by Tim Pfau

—for Muhammad Ali

'There's a hole in the world tonight',
like an empty door from which no one
can come, hollowed space in the middle
of what his solidness had stoppered,
a featureless aperture on tops of heads
like a hole in a roof. There's a hole
where Ali was, a black hole in this space
out-of-bounds to a-holes. He was our ace
in the hole. And so we jazz, cart his casket
with our feelings up this steep street
of night. Loss found a way to make its home
in us. Let the world mourn its champ,
enough for it to know tomb, catacomb, a measure
of grief's weight, of a fist on a black 'fro comb,
yet still feel comfort in what can't be undone.
Staves meet to make a coffin that stores
the body of a spirit, like a vat, or oak casks
with the breath of peat in them. The angel
will come for its share. Our relief lies in this:
though pain is here, we fight to send it back.

Para todos los gatos negros

It has not been known for inns to bury their dead,
even when death occurs inside the establishment;
in the morning, after having brought people in
by the wheel-barrow the night before, the owner
shoos them away, takes back his music
and his drinks from them, and accepts
no accountability for where they are buried,
nor by whom. Even the seediest musician
who slouches over his instrument is killed,
with not even God filled with remorse at all,
but only the furniture and walls left standing.
Dark drapes hang like capes from the ceiling.
The origin of this is so unknown no one, master
who serves lyrics in big portions, or listener
who fills the floor's night, knows why or how
words choose each other when the music
begins, in the sound of the voice of a poet—
but they do, every line with its grain of life.

Last night died before we had given it thought,
but still I wish I'd confessed to poets whose sound
is ideas that alight above people's heads,
or fire night; I have not picked out whom
to yield to, behind my bottle, of this night jazz
which holds my head. Above the crypt, as poems
fly below, a buzz is heard moving with the sound
of a thousand zippers yielding at once.
Words from pen and from mouth
like dew from tips of blades of life, saints
are present, in the vault of this rue Jean-Pierre
Timbaud café, poking wounds with zeal to stop
them healing, each a flat-paper mapper
of a life unknown till then, each charting a world,
the way giving birth turns old life into new.

The fall people

Night after night trees fill the garden
With song, the sound of their words spoken
To spread leaves over the sleeping land
Till all that is nature has awoken,
Note after note, three-fingered gingkos pale
At the tips, blue oaks near the middle peel
In the sun, elephant baobabs with small heads
That even the hand of God could not fell
Try to touch the sound of today's pure breeze.
A bare maple's broad leaves were collected
And used to hide the pain of sin, in this garden
Where useless grace on the central apple tree
Rears its splendid head, and nothing comes of it,
Not even fruitlets shrunk like dry sacs. A family
Once traipsed out of here toward the desert,
Where they say grains of sand lodged each
In their eyes, until those eyes cried, and oil
Appeared at the middle of their oysters. That fruit-
Less land took them thus, with their first sin still
In them, packed it inside a goat, and wrote
Their names off before welcoming them in.

Jamyang

The walls listen from inside the heart's core
beside the temple of a world
whose tanks shut down to a halt,
held back by one who battles nude,
a man who dances with engines
and makes it his duty to foil their intent.
Jamyang sings as if already home,
one chord first, then another one,
music from scriptural papers
etched by monks in words that grow in us
when we remember Amdo, and take
a swastika from the brain. Half the time
the picture is blurred from start
to finish. I'd like to go once to her snows
with a vow which only a single man
may carry, and arrive there, and give her
news that the world is waiting inside,
and marry her with a single heart,
change my name and love the way
she strums a guitar, and believes our life.

Note: Jamyang Kyi, reporter, musician, and TV annouuncer, was
arrested at her office on 1 April 2008 by Chinese police.

Stoep

On a stoep, a moon
comes to see what is in your hearts,
what sign of life nature makes you feel.
It's dark out. Every night it comes
to watch you look at stars
in giant universes, far-off sounds
that explosions make
but that you do not hear,
like reading someone's lips,
the way liking the girl in a mirror
through a friend who used
to know her, can mark the mind;
I recall a day in August
when rain scuttled you both
under a tree, her dress gusting
like a parachute.
And I wished I knew
more than just a little
of the red, inner
lining of that dress.

Our father, who art in heaven

After our father died, his coffin
before nation and king, I stood up
and spoke, read a letter from Switzerland
by a man who had given him his first job
in Morija. People filed past the casket
with its body warmed by the sun.
One told mum to go ahead and weep,
'weep sister,' he said, 'for the man
you have lost.' The water of that day
was the blood of antiquity in the way
it clothed and made us people once
more. We had become, in the space
of a time of grieving, boys, girls,
following a dead man's soul
as we accessed after that day
our images of photos in youth.
I tell all the girls that I am Ben.
But Ben lies in a double-breasted suit
in his room of wood underground.
We all share his nose, eyes, emotion,
crinkly hair, and his slight complexion.

The room of books

Every face carries the strife it possesses, and people
wear these like masks to hide the inside of their colour.
You'll see them sometimes, when the dolour of life
is heavy and unbearable, turn away into the confines
of another street. Some wear them against the weather,
like a hat, or a rubber coat, or a pair of old gumboots.
I wear mine like the sun to burn the things that make me,
the tough sinews of resolve, this hide that has taken me
half to where the bulk of me always wanted to go.

My grandmother used to say a face has failed that has
no baggage under its eyes, to show to others things
that come with age, and feed the choices of the sage,
which are what we rely on. These things fashion you
and turn you into the mission your parents had in mind
for you, before you were born. I remember when she came
to live with us, and my father told us to ask her anything
we could think of, because she was a library. She wore

her face tightly, like a true Basotho dress, and swanked
down the road and up again for all to see what a life lived
looks like in reality. Her posture matched the way
she always felt, about us, and about the way her own son
had turned out. If every smile carries in it the knowledge
of a good world, every sigh knows the solution to part
of what that world is being consumed by. When she died,
a room of rare books and their contents went with her.

Struggles & Home

After the unrest

When we realized it was the beast
and not the ghost, not the face
we had grown so accustomed to
in the years following our struggles
with faith, it was already late; from then on
until this moment we've found ourselves
exposed. Some left their homes
to seek hope in martyrdom.
People hungry for that day ran out
cheering. We gave to mockery
no salvation, no means to secure
its future, which was unusual then;
we went beyond our hour of need.
Spouses fell for each other again
and loved their children more,
because we'd made the city open its arms
and placed in its hands the fondness
we desired, rubbed the gilt off its hair.
When the gathering burst into song,
we knew that the past was gone.

The trouble with country

They inhabit dreams, at night always and on
into day, have severed their cord with earth,
the need for people, preferring to drift alone.
Sunlight avoids their faces. Something deep-intense
hangs above their heads to stir their senses,
but there's no reaction when their knees are knocked;
they wander in themselves; walk where the rush goes
that drives their lives; and they have broken the record
of age like old timers under a village tree. Outside
is nature, forested, sap-ful, black in its posture.
Horny fish swim up a brook as kids in water,
here, outside; the walls are painted with fornication,
which is the religion, our eyeful is not yet blasé, wind
flies lovebirds from bush to bush. Inside… no craft:
they prefer the life the coloniser made, and left. They,
dead inside, are the motherfuckers of the world.

The face of the world

No one knows whether a bird will descend,
or not one bird but a flock, outspread
in their quest for the flesh of broken spirits.
A head bird leads them, slicing air with its wings.
A farmer and his family dash across the fields,
as if the birds could be outrun, or their claws evaded
(no one has ever escaped the laws of nature).
Or as if, upon seeing them, god might decide to mercy
their lot. No one can really say what those birds will do
now, but god who watches them smiles— it's hard,
even for one as high as he, to make such a call.
He leans toward ice because it's apt, a right-now
thing for punishing sloth; but as the almighty
he may, on a whim, opt for something more abrupt,
and loose flames on all who disappoint him.

On the eve of the last day of life,

when the final sun had gone beyond the edge
of its horizon, and even the pinholes of stars
had failed to appear, and no sound but the birr
of a killer drone could be heard approaching
from where village houses had stood earlier,
a mountain reared from the centre of night
and was defined by it. I walked gingerly round it
with eyes closed, with but a path to guide my feet,
blackness all around me, heavy and moist
against my skin, happy in that it had found one
as dark as itself with whom to trek the last miles
of a final distance. The slight path guided me
with how it would lean left or right, or stay even,
onward from the footbridge; or when I crunched
acorns under my feet as I passed the cloister
with its fat oaks where meetings were held.
Among them I wafted, brushing some as I went,
and descended to the valley toward home, where
footpaths know feet which impulsively know
how and what a heart that feeds them feels.

Anger

After festering enough inside her, in bile
which the liver makes each time she remembers
his face, her spell is ready, a spell like a sore.
She swallows more pills every day to destroy
the memory of his name, reads the bible
to find a verse that vilifies him.

One day, while riding him at night,
with his apex rising fast, she unfastened
the knot of his navel and poured
the spell into him, spat in the hole
and re-tied him with a doom.

Kingdom of weeds

The sea has a host of new angels,
not ten miles off the Libyan coast where the boat sank
it carries men in its heart as time carries fate,
and drops them, with the living, on rocks the shore
has prepared for them.

Last night there were voices there,
of lives being changed, those who made it
becoming dead also, to hold their breath
at the bottom and not ever be able to tell their story
to fishermen who talk with waves at night, never explain
how in a dinghy a child is calmed by giving it urine to drink.
They know gods and goddesses of the seabed, now,
who dwell beside Poseidon in his realm of weeds.

Opportunity

Can you hear it, the old man says, his eyes
an open door, or, even, a sky cleared
after fantastic rains. He looks
like a cottage in the countryside
whose thatch roof and picket fence
flourish under the shape of a sun.
Hear what, I ask.
The bus passes empty shelters
between fields of yellow sunflowers
toward a farther end.
The sound of an opening.
I had been coming to the outskirts of the city
since bail. He studied my face
in a way that made me think he knew
my past, like one of his hands
was holding my heart up to the light,
its valves open, its rooms gaping.

I looked back out the window at the houses,
the hills retreating in dread,
trees shaking their heads
and whispering.
The opening, son—
you're in luck. Here, take back
your heart. Stand up now and go
to the front of the bus.
There was no driver!
The old man gave me my heart, told me
there was a job opening for someone
to run my life at last, do I want it?
Then he ducked over a back seat,
disappeared, and was gone.

Sound

A sound beats the skin of my last concern.
Is it a song of life, and is its voice the count
of how much time I have here, vibrant,
making forests and cutting them down, so vile
the sun, on straw hats on heads of people
planting cotton shrubs and ripping their heads off
as this world, and all that is in it, shrugs us off?
The sound says: your worries are like fuel to me,
sit tight because we're shifting into higher gear.
And my head hears cogs grinding,
as the devil and his missus on a sofa grin
like the mouth of a grave swallowing a coffin.
The axle of my body turns on itself though its work
is to hold bones together in a skeleton. I'm a stone
now, I keep the secrets of my heart in, as a furnace
keeps heat in and consumes its own self. O world,
stay your hands from me, stay your heart, because
this sound will sometimes slow down, as a stone
in a brook; and it can rest there, where the hearts
of all birds around it sing and get their ribs
singed by their own song, and little butterflies
flap wings in pursuit of a pheromone. O, I can
stay in there, or I can leap out and bite or gut
your hand with the blade of my life, like the line
a horizon fires when a sun prepares the dawn.

The size of a heart

Many generations have come time and again
and tarried to repair the world, to glue together
pieces of some idyll with that world. In temples
and in synagogues they raise hands in lament,
and snivel and sniffle and plead for penitence.
Yet the child nonetheless dies. That's when earth
shifts from its protracted course to one unknown,
like a captain-less ship, or a sheep separated
from its flock, the holocaust a curse upon it.
A joining has broken, for God will not lift us.
Through all this you'll find me on this porch
scratching thoughts down in anapæstic lines,
my love refusing to leave. I'm the one the law
frisked again as a neighbour peeked in the dark
from behind half-drapes; these sit on a heart
that is already heavy with dissent, near the end
of its breath. Will there be time for healing
in some sun-kissed place, when men talk to others,
and the sizes of their hearts plead their favour?
Will there be men feeling for each other the call
of music whose act of beauty is everything? Or
will we go to a twilight that consumes us?

The flow of water

—*for Pamela Mordecai*

Words come off the page beautifully
and you don't care why it is so, you have
your books in the attic, and also some
on shelves. The dream you have
you support with them, and to yourself
say again how perfect a thing the world is,
and find, in fact, terrific love,
so that on Sunday you relax and sit
and consider everything life
offers. You'll look back on this day
and smile, knowing which way a bridge
sways in a breeze, how still it should stay
when bearing weight, why we must focus
on future cantilevers every day, sturdy
their edges with beams, put them in place,
and screw and paint their nuts and bolts.
You will learn to say nothing to no one,
will make none see or feel or taste this,
nor obsess on how to cross a river
under a rainbow. You'll study water
and know how it makes you feel, how you
must change, because once you dig
a foundation, that is your beginning.

Legs of mangrove trees

Is it standard to have a slave
in a mansion of iron, while
devils & gods have the world
at their feet? Nigger, this
is no Niger—you are where
they want you, to do whatever
they can't do. So the heathens
have achieved their objective
to have you believe in their
personal Eden. & so you go
under the legs of mangrove
trees like when as a child you
saw them come out of the sea.
& you never seek anything
but what is you, which nobody
can take away; & you dance,
& laugh, & play. When it is time
you rise, when all the dogs have
lost your scent, start working
the whole day long in order to be
stronger; &, maybe then, free.

Going home

When in December I leave the cold of Europe
the way men leave their wives to return home,
and arrive there, by car, from the new Mangaung road,
the sun making love to the people again, I'll speed
to my mother; then to the Sunday-clad orchard
behind the house. Some said we would forget each other,
they said out of sight out of mind. But my heart
bulges red like your fruit. On that day's twilight
when the sun goes over the mountain I'll sit
across the table from my mother and hold her hands.
The rust of Lesotho throws itself into dusk; will it
become at dawn what kingdoms should bask in?

—*16 December 2014*

Christmas in Maseru

I have come home, where windows
are shut because the rooms are resting,
each with the memory of life in it; footfalls
sometimes leave one and enter another
across the corridor, whose air is stale. I recall
my father walking there at night, leaning
against the arm of walls to his bedroom,
moved by having his children at home.
When was the last time that had happened?
His memory was fading, but it still waited
each year for the next Christmas; and as usual
he would tell us to gather the cattle,
and based on the reflex of a father's instinct,
pointed one out for the sacrifice. Village men
came with knives, women with tin vessels
in which to milk and rinse the entrails
for the hors d'œuvre. Church is still a usual
thing, and at our altar the Lord Jesus stands
and is baptised with Senqu water by national
hands joined in union. Just Ubuntu, of course,
which says that home is where rivers of love
leave their source and travel to their ocean.

Leaving home

The slow, soft rain beats on the head of my last days
in Maseru, my mother and I sit across the table
talking about another year. There is no animosity
toward nature, as there was none against the sun
of a few days before. We have forgiven. We said it
out loud while looking at each other: 'We forgive'.
I think that sanity is light emanating from her eyes.
When I gaze out the window all I see is tomorrow,
when this rain will be gone and the sun, too, stars
which spent last night falling, as if this day needed
fireworks. No, tomorrow must come. It is day turned
upside-down to show what hides within, a handbag
shaken onto a table and its contents studied. I found
a long lost Parker pen, dry at the nib. I've made a note
to buy a bottle of ink. My mother found a lipstick
she didn't even know she had ever had, and put it
on, our hands searching among old and new objects
in quietness. Somewhere out there water took
a badly placed object, maybe a drum, and rolled it
down the street. A torrent was brewing. I knew
I was searching for what could never be, when you
want to be in two places at the same time. My hand
moved over my mother's and found peace in that.

—*28 December 2014*

Stopping at Japan's place

Hearts aren't meant to be filled up like gas tanks
but to be fulfilled. When the car raced up the Free State
beside its shade, past the first signs of Mangaung
and into Frans Rumpff street, my friend's home
opened its arms to me. Later, as we sat over a drink,
I marvelled at how little damage the years had done.

Booze didn't enter our heads till we started talking
about the ones who are gone, ghosts of the world
in our carcass. And memory comes fast: if people died
in the lobby of this moment how can we lose?
I put my hands behind my head and closed
my eyes to that, to the sound of a dead world.

—29 December 2014

Dinner in the garden

We preferred to have dinner in the garden,
On a wicker table and chairs in the orchard
Under the trees, to smile when saying, 'pass
The salt, please,' looking at a disparate sun;
With father in prison, my brother sat at the head,
Called the menu. The only thing we had to bring
Was furniture and salt. My brother didn't know
That while mom put him at the head she was also
Telling him how to sit, how to pick the salt up
And how much of it to sprinkle. When father got out
We were sick of raw fruit and vegetables. No one
Could look at a beet anymore. We were tired
Of the smell of beef from neighbours' kitchens.
Every morning, even as we washed ourselves
With Lifebuoy we looked at them scrubbing
Oily pots and pans, before we smeared ourselves
With aloe vaseline and made ready for school.

Family reunion

In the afternoon I gather fruit that drops
from our tree; the peach I pick for dad
breaks in my hand and bleeds over my fingers
because it's ripe and sallow, like bushman skin
under the sun of Taung. I pluck one for mum
from a low-hanging branch, and put it
in a different basket, for it's still firm.
I'll put it in a bowl on the kitchen table
and watch as it ripens. Siblings fall
from other trees that a breeze stirs:
this weekend we're having a reunion.
Cousins too, their apricots and prunes
and marete-a-makula touch and kiss
as I carry the heavy baskets to the house,
after which I proceed to shave and shower,
put on a clean shirt. There are friends
already in the house, from Ha-Tšiu outside
town, and from as far as Bloemfontein.
I knot my tie, fix my hair with a 'fro comb
dad never let us use. The mirror smiles.
I rub my eyes, dad is staring back at me.

Life is family

—said by Yolisa

The sun enters by the back window and crosses our rooms
on its way to another side. I pull the covers over myself
to hide from it, but life is persistent and it makes me get up.
I eat my porridge, and toast, at the table with the big people,
but I brush my teeth alone afterward. The walk to school
is a happy affair. I enjoy the music in the voices of everyone
I run into, greeting the world and everything in it; the whole
day, I know, their voices will sound in my head: *Lumelang!*
And, *Sawubona!* When I get back home the sun will have long
left my room, on its way to someone else's house on the other
side of the world. I gloat in the way we share it, and I know
that mama will have left a sandwich or scones for my after-
school snack. And as I eat them, the words she always says,
'I'll see you tonight, baby,' replace the twitter of morning
chatter. My father says *'Tsamaea hantle'* and *'Hamba kahle'*
are like cloth tearing, like teacher's chalk on the blackboard.
He always grits his teeth when he says them. He tells me
that cloth is better when sewn, and chalk when moistened
a little. I love mornings since they help me look forward
to evenings when my parents come back home, because
I know then for sure they've been good and careful at work.
The reason I look forward to morning is I dislike mourning.

Feeding the ground

Out of a boundless kitchen in which life grew up
There's no sound now, but that of intervening years,
A muted hum of men digging, lifting picks
Over their backs and striking, and before morning
A hole is ready in the ground, its mouth gaping
Like a hatchling's waiting for food, as if the cemetery
Were a nest with little mouths to feed, the grim reaper
A parent to those mouths. In my mother's kitchen
Where I learned to sing, the diggers' muffled song
Comes through, hmmm ha home… hmmm ha home,
And again, and again, the beaks of their picks fall.
I once asked my mother why only men dig the ground
At night, and she said 'because men make children
Go.' And she turned around and with a lesokoana
Dug into the papa she was making. 'We feed them.'
Sometimes she'd start a song, or tell a fable. Now,
When I hear the sound coming from the floor,
Or from the graveyard on the left when you go
To Loretto, I think of every nightshift, and of men
Who work it to make sure that the ground is fed.

Against windows of our heart

Run from the altar of their home
they fled to us. Father spoke to them
at the door, then asked them in,
against windows of our heart.
They had driven overnight to come here
because of oppression in their land.
We called them foreign cousins.
My brother fell in love with their daughter
and I, when they left months later,
with the way my parents handled that affair.
One belongs to an altar, a child to its father's house.
It has never been the other way round.
When it was our turn to flee our own home
dad seethed at god, forgetting even then
that altars can't belong. After exile I was me
more than before our need for someone
else's kindness. They talked to my father
at their door, then gently ushered us in.

Nature & Death

Pula

I want rain on this country,
I want it to hit tin roofs of inhabitants
who have waited long
for it, I want rock
slapped like glass buttocks;
and, after all, a foot-dance
near the fields, to honour water.
I want kids to build boats
and send them on voyages
across puddles, mud-happy
in the knowledge that shores
await, beyond mountain
or width of river, with tadpoles
that they have dubbed fish.
Vast memoirs of peacelessness
can never console us;
except when there is rain.

The rose

Nothing can ever become a white vase
with a rose in it, red and cut at the stem
on one of our walks along a hill-path
and brought here to impart beauty to our house.
On Sundays they sell roses at the market
for five bop a bunch. But they're tame shadows
of this one and have been neutered, their nails
clipped, their dreads trimmed. Their souls taken
from them. But not this bitch's. We had gone
up the hill on an instant feeling to find her;
and that's when my wife saw her, hiding beside
the ledge of a feldspar, near a clump of bushes
which only the eye of a keen passer-by could
have discerned. She yanked her head back
when she spotted us, but it was too late,
I'd already pulled my toolkit out, a Swiss army knife
I got last Christmas, and was inching across the rock
to get to her. That day, lunch was a fast affair.
For the rest of it she kept stealing glances at us
and scowling. My wife took her a glass of water
and they talked, woman to woman, and brushed
each other's sepals with small, soft hands,
till the petals of both blushed again and again.

Sea hunger

During an August that was wet with rain
after El Niño had passed there in a huff,
the sea was hungry. And, though long
after its water had gulped the boy, his parents
visited that beach each summer, its water
refused to give him back. These lands belonged
to it, inherited from rivers that crawl here to die,
the way elephant cemeteries belong to the mammoth
family and Sioux lands ought to still be Sioux, native
as England. It gritted its teeth through years
and ignored flowers they placed at its feet.
Year after year they came with roses and dahlias,
and wild violets of the kind picked on walks
along the water edge by people with heavy hearts.

When the boy was twenty-one the ocean put him
on its lap and asked him how old he was. The boy,
who was bright, said, 'I have watched the backs
of fish glint upward and called it morning, seen
their bellies dim on the way down, and called it
evening. That's how I marked my days; and for each
I dropped a bottle for day and a tin or plastic bag
for night under the overhanging rock.' And he led
the way to his trove of rubbish whose days together
they counted, two-by-two-by-two, to twenty-one
years. That summer, when the parents approached
the shrine, the sea spat the boy back onto the beach,
asked a gust to dry him off, and retired to its lair.

Syzygy

—written with Joyce Ellan Davis

Last night's blood moon came, then went,
leaving us like a bunch of jilted brides
stranded at the altar. It was red, and also rusty
with the high tide, like a dream in oxidation,
the standard link of bodies on a rhapsody.
Death that the early scientist meant with words
a committee archived inside the belly of Rome.
But there we were, ready for rapture to a rented room
in a Motel 6, willing, like Isaac, like a thousand
immaculate virgins whose lamps have gone out.
I thought of Einstein, of Kepler and of all masters
whose world bends and falls. I thought of me
upon a lost, irritable earth. It was just a moon,
but no thought stayed from it, not one mantra
nor the preaching of men to hold it down,
or make it stop. In the minutes that shadowed us
as it floated across, the caveman resuscitated,
circling a fire and singing, like only he could,
about how last night's blood moon came and went;
till all was nearly deathly, then ashen, till it turned
the corner of day to update us on how we will be
in the time behind all absence from our world.

—October 2015

Walking woman
—written with Amanda R. Morgan

There is a moment in August when the cicada song
inches up in pitch and is sung as a single note:
one big hum that wasn't there before.
There are many things in summer that make my heart sing,
but when I hear their sound, it breaks with the joy
of an angel choir at night. There is nothing in summer
that heat can't melt, nor rainfall wash off, nor dew at the tips
of a morning freeze, except the song of cicadas in August—
that alone was written on me as in stone, imagoes on trees,
indivisible from bark. It is not red poppies in the breeze,
nor fruit so ripe and so russet it thuds to the ground,
unable to hang on, nor backyard fires at family braais,
it is none of these; and if this world in its diversity
were to just stop at the same time across the globe, just
not make a sound for once, then these imago
songs would fill everyone with the joy that I feel always
when they shift from pitch to pitch in harmony with
things.

What this is

—written with Jo Hemmant and Cora Greenhill

is I could never tire of looking at the sky,
at the way gold creeps up and becomes blue
when day has got a footing on our lives again,
or white, across the hands of unsuspecting trees,
the minute a world feels it needs shade,
or Jove thinks it does, or wind and water
in a combination of effort that hoists and uplifts,
the blood of chlorophyll rolls its sleeves up
and pushes our grave ideology into the sea.
I watch people walk beneath that shade home
after a day in the sun, or rain, or in a box
under glass roofs of our time, till they arrive
where minutes, hard-won, slip through orange-red
outside closed doors, blinds drawn, to the pulse
of stars. Certain curtains are swept back at dawn.
This is when the fallen rise, and swarm space
from hive to hive. This is when a sudden crowd
of starlings makes a gamble to dance, as on
through aging minutes it paints air out of air.
This is where denial stops, and a glacier
has the right to diminish, where time is allowed
revolt, where the inklings of itself are the start.

World at night

It is not late to pause here
and listen to these woods, to lake-water
lapping the shore. A light wakes
in one of the flats overlooking the park,
it is late for the deck chair left outside
for those who cannot bear to dream
but will wander through boundless night.
It is not late for bats to come out
and fluster the night through; no doubt
it is a plan to make the world a bitter place.
I believe in things sense will have me know,
us as beasts christened in sex to attest
each day of hunger in the mouth. If it's time
to let one feeling out, let me make myself
whatever I can of this moment, put false-
hood behind, let mercy be judge.

Weather report

Soon after the sky had struck two rocks against each other
darkness dropped a stack of porcelain plates, turned trees
upside down, swept the country with them, even
as my brother, the youngest one who was born
at independence, sat on my shoulders and wept for the sun
till the lines of his brow had become deep as dongas.

Tobacco has long yellowed my sister's teeth, though
she still spends everyday on the stoep knitting gold threads
into a sunhat, or rolling a zol to blow puffs that will chase
bad clouds away. The mat she sits on is frayed at the edges
but my sister refuses to have it exchanged, the same sister
who made a child, only to see it dismantled in three years.

They say that village children are scared to come and sing
the 'Mankokosane song, that they've all gone home;
but rain's hegemony is done. Besides, here comes dawn
down the slope past the outcrop where we used
to gambol when we were teens, dawn with a hamper
of plenty in one hand, another of karma in the other.

News

—for my uncle, Nthaha

The news came by wire in the morning,
as I sat to start the business of the day:
he is dead! They say in Maseru trees
refuse to line streets, they have taken
a keen liking to revolution, and bring it
alive through the dark bark of their skin.
As you drive by you see them protesting
with placards. At night they'll stand there
and refuse to sleep. Throughout seasons
a cry will reach faces of people going by,
who will die too, like him, when it is time.
Children hang at corners in search of work,
but Maseru has no work for them. Its schools
are tombs of the unknown student, rooms
aching for the one who is dead. But the thrill
of this town is rain that comes, after washing
the highlands, and in movement greets plough-
pusher and the woman with a clay pail on
her head, to let them know that he is dead,
and is not alive. Such rain will not reach
those like me who are far from home, who
cry in the cupped room of their hands,
which before held god but not any more.

Preparing the body

—for my uncle, Nthaha

He's dead; in Oort, the gods know.
As the news leaves press rooms
eels, from the bottom of the Aegean,
ribbon to the surface to wave goodbye;
we smear his body with Zambuk
and wash the rotted parts with milk,
parts that are known as the devil's cut.
His wife washes between the legs
then returns later to put the legs straight
again, before the thigh muscles stiffen.
This is why a man must die before his wife.
At the edge of the open grave I pretend
to be a man, and proceed to find a stone
I spit on, then throw into the hole.
This is how a man accompanies relatives
on the journey out of life. People look
around with downcast faces, longing
for a different chemistry of sleep.

One of my memories is that you returned

with a bullet in the middle of yourself,
explaining how days should never be trusted
with a secret, how it was clear the sun no longer
shone with feeling. So I said to the future:
this is no good, what of you will remain for the world?
'We will waste no more of your time,' I said.
But it just smiled with its grey eyes and looked away,
for it knows death is a gruesome business
that hits when one is down. Its stillness
was like air. Even if life is knowing, your body
will always be as calm as the mind of a sea
which may rise in anger only to simmer down—
what two tell each other is a matter for them,
while talking about what shadow they should need,
afterwards, when death has found them out.

A door that refuses to open

Rain has been pouring down for various days
and has washed blood that dappled our doorstep,
which even soap and brushes could not get out,
it clung to that place where the boy had ebbed
and would not let go. Even my mother got down
on her knees one day with a *tjale* around her waist
and rolled her sleeves up, the way she does to knead
dough, and scrubbed and scrubbed, and finally lost
every hope of ever calming the anger of that night.
Dirt had soon drunk most of it on that morning
it happened, but splodges had remained, one after
another, on the steps leading to the house
(like the footsteps of our government visiting prey),
daring us to detach them. We were a death-home
within the village of breathing houses. It was blood
with a smell like rusted iron, against rain that came
and wouldn't leave (uttering not one word, except
a constant drum-drum of its fingers on our roof)
I could imagine some face of pain, but in the dark
who could attest to having seen a thing like that?
A door thinks it must remain shut along its length
and bottom to keep spirits inside, where folks lie,
so they can comfort us in our sleep, and later go
where they came from through an open window.
That night they left through our toothless door.

Commandments

Memory lifts its veil, everybody calls you,
but no appearance. Once again I recall
walking nights with you, touching walls
toward a light of home's distance
lit for those still outside, till that night
became another day. I remember ten
childhood commandments, how absent
loves have to be watered and fed with half
the force of touch, with light, and a tongue,
and half with a winter of wild surmise.
Today still the quiet night brings images
of walking toward that hill of home,
using darkness as a guide there. Then
one morning you were gone, on one day
that took you away, your stature, the slight
non-form of your build—for all that was you—
none of us knew what was coming despite
what you embody today. What we had not
realised was that there was no ram tied
to Abraham's shrub. Thou shalt not awake
after dying, thou shalt be willing to refuse
refuge in the arms of their Lord. You left
Lesotho the year of your eighteen years
and we closed our eyes. Grass grew a beard
on you, and thou shalt 'get up, stand up'
rang the air. These are not on any tablet
but on the skin of our hearts. Because thou
shalt not hate nor rape thy neighbour, and
thou shalt aid people, thou shalt worship
other Gods beside me. These many years
afterward you remain needed. Because thou
shalt never leave loved ones in the lurch.

Reasons for killing a child in his sleep

—after Chris van Wyk

It was dark, and the gun was distracted.
The distracted gun was dark. And it was
The gun, it was distracted and was dark,

Therefore I couldn't see straight enough.
Enough, therefore! I couldn't see straight.
Couldn't I therefore see straight enough?

Someone else was meant for that death,
For death meant someone was that else,
Else that death was meant for someone.

His mama used him as a human shield,
A shield used him as his human. Mama
Used a shield, his mama, human as him.

Struggles among men are blind and cruel,
And among men cruel struggles are blind,
Cruel men are blind and among struggles.

I did not mean to kill him, your honour.
Did I not, your honour, kill to mean him?
Not your kill, I did mean to honour him.

For Kananelo

My sister left home for a kid,
if a world could trace itself against those
who walk it. Then she came back with

a boy, and it was like driving Time
from the rafters and sweeping the hut
out with mohlomo brooms,

shaking sheets and beating mattresses
outdoors on Saturday with a stick.
The thing about that boy was we loved

his face, which was dark. Strange
that we loved him thus, even though
no one knew he was but passing through.

My sister's boy

The day my sister's boy was born
she poured honey and whiskey
into a pan, stirred warmed palm oil in,
mixed them with her hands several times,
then smeared it all over the boy's body.
'This is how I will love you', she said,
as if to herself, her hands
rubbing his groin and buttocks, tickling
his toes. He studied her awhile
and giggled, then stuck a thumb
into his pink mouth and sucked it
with his eyes closed.
'It's exactly how I will love you, baby'.
Someone ran outside and fixed
a white flag onto the roof to announce
the birth. Women came with pails
of home brew. Someone sacrificed a bull.
Still we had to wait and wait for rain
in order to place the infant out
and leave him there till he toughened,
enough to take the name the tribe would place
in him. He smelled the air and smiled.

The consequence of life

Right after my dad died, and our heads were nude,
and black cloth was pinned to our shirt sleeves,
even before any heaven had dried our eyes,
the body of my mother became a question mark,
though there were no answers to be found at all.

Before we had taken the cognizance which death imparts,
she was shuffling from room to room twinkling at us,
seeking chores, unpacking this and repacking that,
handling garments which had taken the naphthalene
of their hearts and smeared it on her fingers,
like some secret charm between them. Part of it

she remembered from portions of her mind,
but the rest came at her afresh everyday in greater
proportions, and ripped all we didn't know she had.

We got her a walking stick to lift her off earth,
because a fecund plant must stay off the ground
if it wants to live, if it will accept the chance
to bear more fruit still. Mother started taking steps
one by one to the top of her stairs, where memory
lay stocked, then walked slowly back down again
from her journey into the past, back to the level
of the living. Maseru's terrain scoffs at the low sea.

Mother's children, and piles of books and photos
stacked in her mind's attic, keep her here and alive;
and death? I've seen dreams of people thrilled by it.

Father died a modern one, with tubes of highways
in his face, but with no trace at all, in those eyes,
of sorrow, or anger, at things humans do to others.

The martyr

Throughout winter
we looked forward to spring,
and planned how we would enjoy it
once it finally came round,
till those men slaughtered the boy,
which set us back more than a season
at least. They took what they could
from what remained of his heart
and split—just like that—
though not before
they had lifted their leg
on the way out, and pissed
like a dog on the inner walls
of his heart, in both the atria
and the ventricles, and stopped
one eventual time at the door
to spit on his ancestral name.

Fenstere

The large window of our house
still watches the world
from the vantage of its hill,
following the events of September
1981. It sees passers-by and shines itself
at them like a tinsel in the sun,
and when night falls it feels remorse
at what it has seen, and goes to sleep
with its eye open, like a fish, or a rabbit,
ready for a fight or for flight, the same way
a horse sleeps on its feet. That window
would not have been that big
if we had known the world
would also look in. From the street
people turned their heads and glared
at it. Yet we would not have seen
the storm had the window not been as large.
One day we shall put an eyelid on it,
to help it rest at night, or blink in surprise
when people go against the teachings
of themselves. We shall look at it, then,
and love it again for keeping to itself
the secret lives of fornicaters and thieves
and the identity of the men who came
that spring after a midnight in September
and rat-tatted the whole village awake,
and rat-tatted the body of a boy away.

The question of Mokema

—for Maaparankoe

Wild eggs of the ostrich lie about like skulls.
At night, when no one is looking, and Lesotho
pauses to yawn… rub its eyes with its fists,
the killer and his men put down their guns
to plan a new slaying. At the thought, hawks
flock out of trees and head to the kopjes for safety.
The only other cry is the groan of water,
above the one an old owl makes
with its questions: 'who… who… who?'
But there's no reply from inside the faces
of these men, though new fear grips the land.
How we shall miss you, our country. Leisure
is dead in the eye. Nobody laughs anymore.

Acknowledgements

Mention must be made here of the following mentors, publishers, editors, readers, muses, commenters and co-authors, all of whom have influenced the contents of this book in one way or another.

Amanda R. Morgan
Botsotso
Canopic Jar and Canopic Publishing
Chris van Wyk
Christina Seymour
Cora Greenhill
David Barnes
David Caddy
Emma Nobuntu Mbelebele & Yolisa
Geoffrey Philp
Helen Moffett
Jo Hemmant
Joyce Ellen Davis
Julia F. Cooper
Lieutenant-General Maaparankoe Mahao
Malik Crumpler
Michelle McGrane
Motlatsi Masilo
Motlatsi Mpobole
My parents, siblings, wife, and children
Pamela Mordecai
Pansy Maurer-Alvarez
Peter Midgley
Phil Rice
Rustum Kozain
Spoken Word Paris
Tears in the Fence
Tim "TJ" Pfau
Tuesday Poem
and Virginia Smith Rice

Thank you

About the Author

Rethabile Masilo blogs at Poéfrika and co-edits *Canopic Jar*. He is a Mosotho poet from Lesotho and has lived in Paris, France, since 1987. His work has been published in various anthologies as well as hard and soft-copy magazines, including *Canopic Jar, The Bastille, With Our Eyes Wide Open, Seeing the Unseen, Tears In The Fence, New Coin, Botsotso, Badilisha Poetry*, and others. In 2014 his poem "Swimming," published in *New Coin Poetry*, Vol 49, N°1, won the Dalro First Prize. The same poem won the Thomas Pringle Award for Poetry in Periodicals in 2015. He has also edited two anthologies published by The Onslaught Press: *For the Children of Gaza*, and *To Kingdom Come* (voices against political violence).

Rethabile was born in 1961 in Lesotho and left his country with his parents and siblings to enter exile in 1981, following an attack on his family that killed his 3-year-old nephew, Motlatsi. They moved through the Republic of South Africa, where they experienced Apartheid; Kenya; and the United States of America before settling in France.

In 2012 his first book of poems, *Things That Are Silent*, was published by Pindrop Press. The second book, *Waslap*, was published in 2015 by The Onslaught Press. *Letter to Country* is his third collection. He insists that his greatest wish is for his poems, and poetry in general, to be readily available to Basotho, the people who inspire him to write.

www.ingramcontent.com/pod-product-compliance
Lightning Source LLC
LaVergne TN
LVHW091230080426
835509LV00009B/1235

9 780997 169522